This book is presented to

---

by

ON YOUR OWN BUT NOT ALONE

Life After College

WILLIAM H. WILLIMON

DIMENSIONS
FOR LIVING
NASHVILLE

ON YOUR OWN, BUT NOT ALONE:
Life After College

This book is printed on recycled, acid-free paper.

Library of Congress Cataloging-in-Publication Data

Willimon, William H.
On your own but not alone: life after college/William H. Willimon.
p. cm.
ISBN 0-687-15526-6 (alk. paper)
1. College graduates—Religious life. 2. Christian life—1960-
I. Title.
BV4529.2.W55 1995
248.8'34—dc20 94-19608

95 96 97 98 99 00 01 02 03 04 05—10 9 8 7 6 5 4 3 2 1

MANUFACTURED IN THE UNITED STATES OF AMERICA

To

WILLIAM
and
HARRIET

Contents

Introduction

CAN YOU BELIEVE IT? After years and years of becoming educated for, preparing to enter into, and waiting to commence toward, you are at last graduating! This is your "commencement," your long-awaited step into the "real world." Congratulations!

Are you ready? It's odd, that after waiting so long, after studying so hard, graduation can be a frightening time in your life. When I was at your stage in life, I remember a professor who told me that my college years were "the best years of your life." I remember thinking that he was right. What does that say about the rest of your life? Leaving college friends, departing from the joys of campus life, entering the job market, thinking about marriage, family—it can be scary. Good-bye, college. Lots of luck.

Can I help? I work with people your age every day. As a campus minister, I can assure you that you are not the only graduate in the world to feel excited, but also scared; to feel that you are ready to commence into the world, but also have some doubts about your ability to cope with the world; to feel ready to leave, but also wishing that you might stay. This book is a collection of Christian biblical thoughts, by someone who knows what it's like to begin your life journey as an adult. Read on.

Who will go with you? Recently, an article in *The Wall Street Journal* referred to folks your age as "The Damned Generation." Confronted by a shrinking economy, a skyrocketing crime rate, AIDS, and poor job prospects, many in your generation are feeling cursed, victimized, shortchanged by the future. *On Your Own, But Not Alone* looks at you from a very different perspective. As a Christian, you know something which assures you that, although your world will be a great challenge, it is a world that has been created and loved by God. Although you may have problems and difficulties in your life, you are someone who has been loved, chosen, and gifted by God in Jesus Christ. Therefore, I prefer to refer to you as "The Blessed Generation." God goes with you.

Our expression "Good bye" comes from the old English expression, "God be with you." So when we say "Good-bye college," we're also saying that you are not going alone—God is with you.

As someone who has received the blessing of a prosperous life thus far—the great gift of a good education—you are in a minority of the world's people. You have been greatly blessed. You have been given advantages and opportunities that most of the world's people will never have. Therefore, God has laid a claim upon your life. As Jesus once said, "From everyone to whom much has been given, much will be required" (Luke 12:48). A person with great gifts is called by God for great responsibility. This book is meant to help you both to claim God's gifts and to use those gifts for godly good.

Welcome to the world!

William H. Willimon
Duke University Chapel

1

Go for It!

The LORD is with us; do not fear.
Numbers 14:9*c*

Read Numbers 13:1-2, 17-20, 25-28, 30; 14:4, 6-9.

THERE YOU ARE, preparing to cross another threshold, your graduation into the world. Are you ready to go? There is a malady that sometimes afflicts seniors, called the "There's-still-one-more-course-I'd-like-to-take Syndrome." Strange, people who, in their sophomore year, couldn't find anything worth having in the curriculum, now in their senior year, report that their education can be complete only by taking a few more courses. Can I stay another year? No, dear, we say, we've already promised your room to three others. You have to go. Good-bye, *adios*, this is it.

People on the outside are forever asking me, What are today's students like? It's tough to generalize, but I say, well, *scared.* Many of you are scared.

Some 54 percent of you think that life will be worse for you than it has been for us. Only 32 percent think it will be better (*Scholastic Inc.*, 1992). Your pessimism is not unjustified. The new world you are commencing into may not be a promised land, but rather the land of new fears, big hurdles.

Which brings us to a story of explorers of New Worlds. They are at the door to the Promised Land. The forty years of waiting and wandering for these former slaves is about to end. At last they stand on the threshold of this new land, promised to slaves who had nothing. One small problem: The land is already occupied. The place is crawling with Canaanites.

A friend of mine was teaching this text in Texas. Among his students were a number of Native Americans. At first mention of "the Promised Land," a hand went up.

"Yes? What is it, Mr. Running Bear?"

"Who promised the land to the Hebrews?"

"Well, God did."

"Did God tell the Canaanites that he had promised their land to somebody else?"

"Could we move on with the class?"

Moses sends scouts to reconnoiter the land, find out what things are like over there, how big a force will be required to take it. After a few days, the explorers return. There is a majority report. And there is a minority report given by Caleb. And in hearing their reports, we are impressed by the gap in their perception.

"The cities there are utterly impregnable." Here is a land which "devours its inhabitants." What does he mean? We don't know. Is there famine? Surely not with those gigantic grapes! Disease? War?

"The people over there are like giants [literally, 'Sons of the long neck']," they said. "Compared to them, we are like *grasshoppers!*"

The people over there—they have a great educational system, don't do drugs, work hard at the factory, and eat diets low in saturated fat. Why, compared to them, our people look like grasshoppers! The people went crazy with fear when they heard this majority report.

"What have you done," they screamed at Moses, "to bring us all the way out here only to perish at the hands of those industrial giants? At least in Egypt, we knew our place and had three square meals a day!"

"But you were *slaves,*" said Moses.

"Well, we had it better in the safety of slavery than out here where we're food for these Canaanite giants. We might have lived like grasshoppers in Egypt, but we were well fed grasshoppers."

Then came the minority report: Caleb said, "I can't believe we saw the same place. This land is rich. The Lord is with us. It's ours for the taking. Let's go at once and take what the Lord has given us."

Here the threshold of the Promised Land, graduation from slavery to freedom, is rendered as a dilemma. Who shall name the future—the fearful majority, or the faithful minority? We know this story well—that every journey's end is an invitation to a new, and perhaps more perilous, path. Every victory lands us on the edge of the unknown. At the threshold between a land we knew and one we do not know, between the grinding, dehumanizing world of the slave and the risky, unknown, promised world of free land, a great deal depends upon how we describe our dilemma.

The majority saw the Promised Land only as Canaan, land of impregnable fortresses, unscalable heights, and invincible enemies. But Caleb spoke of Canaan as God's land, land of God's promise, to give as God pleased. He even spoke of the Canaanites as God's people. Could they have been describing the same place? A vast, epistemological, theological gap lies between "They are giants; we are grasshoppers" and "God is with us. Let us go forth."

Now, I'll admit that this story is a risky tale to tell—so risky that I had thought it best not tell it, for fear of the damage it could do if poorly told. This has been the Bible story used by the possessors of land, to justify how they got it and why they must retain it with murderous possessiveness. This is the story of Columbus in 1492, of Cortez, and of Custer ("God is with us. Let us go forth."). In calling what was really a very ancient world the "New World," we became giants in our own eyes and treated millions of God's people like grasshoppers. There are no Canaanites' voices in the 1492 story, for our history has not heard the cries of the vanquished.

But I am hoping that you can see how such a telling is an ideological perversion of this story, rather than the actual story. This story makes sense only by being a constant reminder that it was told first by a *landless* people. The people who told this empowering tale were slaves, and before that, nomads, people who had never known the promise of land. This is a tale told in the ghetto, at the bottom, in the barrio, at the refugee camp, a tale meant to electrify those who have nothing, but who are imaginative enough to believe the promise that this is God's world and that God intends them to have it.

Scholars believe that this story of Moses, Caleb, and the explorers took its place in Numbers sometime after 721 B.C., with the collapse of the Northern Kingdom. Israel had been devastated by Assyria, had lost its land and therefore its future.

How did such a national disaster occur? Numbers asserts that it happened due to lack of faith in God. Other explanations were possible—a weak military system, bad education, the failings of the younger generation. Numbers says it had to do with a widespread inability to trust a living God, the failure to live Caleb's "God is with us. Let us go forth."

Question: Can this story told to the landless speak to the landed? You and I are not in a ghetto, a barrio. We are the beneficiaries of an expensive education. Many of us are here, in great part, because we have been the possessors of all that this society has to offer—the best homes, best schools, best advantages. And we like to think that we are where we are because we took advantage of our advantages. "God is with us. Let us go forth."

But is there no part of us able to admit that most of what we have came to us as *gift?* Do we believe it? Do we believe that what we have was *God's* before it was ours?

And is there no part of us able to be surprised—having been assured since 1492 that we are landed, titled, entitled, secure, gifted—that this could be a lie, the hype of a society more internally troubled than it dares admit to its young?

Odd to find ourselves, five hundred years after Columbus, feeling so old in this allegedly New World, our little North American noses pressed to the shop window, peering at other nations' material achievements, coming to feel like the dispossessed in the technological/industrial world we created?

For if we can imagine ourselves not as lords of all we survey, but as frail, unsteady, scared emigrants on the threshold of a future we may not control, then and only then may this old story speak to us.

Part of you may want to go back to Egypt, to the narrow, but at least secure, world we once had. Don't go back, for back there is slavery, not life. You may think your future will be smaller than your parents' past and present. Most of you do not expect to make as much or to live as well as your parents. No wonder you worry! But I predict that your future will be not just smaller, but different, maybe even better. For from my brief expeditions into your generation, I like what I see. Your student generation has been known for its spirit of volunteerism, cleaning up the mess your parents have made of their cities, the public schools, and health care, one person at a time.

In a weird way, you are going into the Promised Land, though it looks a good deal different, and maybe even better, than the land your parents thought God had promised to us.

Put aside your fears. Go for it! *Not* because you're smart, talented, gifted (though many of you may be). No! Because "*God* is with us. Let us go forth."

2

Dreams and How to Keep Them

To these four young men God gave knowledge and skill in every aspect of literature and wisdom; Daniel also had insight into all visions and dreams.

Daniel 1:17

Read Daniel 1.

CONGRATULATIONS! You are now a college graduate! At last you have arrived at the place of your dreams, the real world.

But now comes the tough part, because the world sometimes is a tough place for youthful dreams.

"It's weird," he said.

"What's weird?" I asked.

"Weird how they give you a bid to join their fraternity, get you to pledge and then, beginning on the night you pledge, they try to make you into somebody else. They say they want you to join because they like you. But then, 'Get an attitude,' they'll tell you. 'Drink this,' 'do that.' "

I remember, as a young professor, when the Dean called me in and attempted to reassure me concerning my upcoming appearance before the tenure committee. "Don't worry," the Dean said. "I see no problems ahead for you on the vote."

I told him I wasn't worried. I felt as if I had been through the whole thing before.

"Been through it before?" the Dean asked.

"Yes. Pi Kappa Alpha. Voted into the brotherhood. Of course, there they judged you on qualities like the color of your socks or the clothes you wore. Here they judge you on the articles you write and the color of your socks. But it's all the same."

I'm saying there's a price for fitting in. Sometimes it will cost your dream.

What resources can help you resist? I shall tell you an old, old tale of resistance. The story of Daniel was told, we believe, by Jews, to sustain hope and confident resistance during their persecution under Antiochus (c. 175 B.C.).

The story begins far from home, in Babylon, in exile. Think of exile as being a freshman, alone, far from home. Babylon is a metaphor for empire—for large, militarily based, universally sanctioned power—Nebuchadnezzar. Nobody is bigger than King Nebuchadnezzar—not the Jews, not their God. The play opens with the temple destroyed and the Jews as powerless exiles.

King Nebuchadnezzar has his chief of staff, Ashpenaz, bring him a few talented, good looking Jewish boys to be educated for court service (v. 3). See? Nebuchadnezzar isn't such a bad king after all. From among the slaves, Nebuchadnezzar generously offers a few Jewish boys upward mobility. Tokenism? No. He has thought up a government student-aid program. He will enable these Jews to make good on imperial terms.

The story says that they are without spot or blemish, scored high on the SAT, full of learning and understanding, destined to lead, just the sort of people pursued by the big corporations and law schools. They are to be cared for, pampered, given the best education the empire has to offer, in a three-year executive training program (v. 5).

Sound familiar? The boys are named Daniel, Hananiah, Mishael, and Azariah, but I think you know them!

And while these lucky young people are being groomed for greatness, they are put on a special executive diet. They're not going to eat with common rabble, victims of the college cafeteria; no, they will be given "royal rations of food and wine" (v. 5). They will know which fork to use, what to do with a lobster, executive food.

An executive recruiter for a large corporation told me that, in selecting prospects, he always takes them to dinner at a fancy restaurant. "You can tell if someone is executive material, by the way that person eats."

Note that nothing has been said about conformity. Nothing ever is said about conformity when the empire is conforming you to its appetites and manners. Capitulation begins when young people are being told that they are "the best and the brightest," privileged for special treatment. Nothing is coercive. It doesn't need to be coercive. All that's needed, in the path to conformity, is our natural desire to fit in.

Thus we are surprised in the story when told that "Daniel resolved that he would not defile himself with the royal rations of food and wine" (v. 8). In Babylon, nobody made such a fuss over food. Diet was no big deal. They weren't fanatics. But Daniel quietly rejects imperial beef for Jewish vegetables. He rejects the royal program for upward mobility, and at this point, God enters the story. "God allowed Daniel to receive favor and compassion from the palace master" (v. 9). The palace master, as a government bureaucrat, little toady that he is, is stunned to meet someone with as much self-confidence as Daniel. He appears to admire him and wants to help. Nevertheless, he is concerned about how the king will react to Daniel's resistance. What if the king notices that the Jewish boys are skinnier than the others?

Daniel proposes a scientific experiment. For ten days, Daniel and his friends will follow their vegetarian diet, while a control group feasts on the king's beef and wine. Result? "At the end of ten days it was observed that they appeared better and fatter than all the young men who had been eating royal rations" (v. 15).

The story tells us that Daniel's amazing act of self-possession and his free, risky, youthful resistance is a *gift* of God. God again enters the story and "gave knowledge and skill in every aspect of literature" (automatic expertise in English Lit.) to these rebellious young men. "Daniel also had insight into all visions and dreams" (v. 17). Nebuchadnezzar finds Daniel and his friends "ten times better than all the magicians . . . in his whole kingdom" (v. 20). We did not know that things would turn out this well at the beginning of the narrative.

Daniel had no guarantee that his risky resistance would be so rewarded. Neither do we. Surprise! By the end of the story we discover that God loves rebels! Bureaucrats, bean counters, good soldiers, writers of rules, lackeys for the Dean of Students bore God. God is with the whistle-blowers, the troublemakers, the young turks. God showed up in only two places in the story: First, to support Daniel's act of dietary resistance. (God loves people whose life goals are more interesting than merely fitting in.) Second, to give Daniel visions, dreams. (God is with the dreamers.)

Unlike those young Jews, we aren't threatened by persecution. Our menace is seduction. The story suggests that the ability to resist depends upon dreams different from the officially sanctioned ones. The story invites young adults to venture out beyond the status quo, the world your elders tell you is fixed reality, to which you must simply adjust. It beckons you out into a world of risk, and gift, where allegiance to our dreams pushes us out to where we need God to sustain us.

Jesus told his people, "When they bring you before the synagogues, the rulers, and the authorities, do not worry about how you are to defend yourselves or what you are to say; for the Holy Spirit will teach you at that very hour what you ought to say" (Luke 12:11-12). God is with the rebels.

Alas, you have arrived at this stage in life on much the same path as I. We're here because we've always been good at fitting in, doing what we were told, adapting. The kid who gave the teacher such a fit in your geometry class—he's not at college commencement. One of the sad functions of "higher education" is to domesticate youthful expectation, to convince you that your identity is mostly a matter of docile adjustment, rather than pushy self-assertion; that those who listen carefully and feed it all back on the exam are smarter than those who have a dream and refuse to relinquish it.

And it is all so well done that you don't know you've been had until you wake up one day at age forty, to find that someone else has always pulled your strings, that there is almost nothing to which you will not stoop, that there is no "you" there anymore. At night, when you close your eyes, you worry about your mortgage, rather than dream dreams. It is all so mundane, caught up in everyday issues, issues such as: Who feeds you? How much will you pay to sit at the right table? And it always begins quite innocently, as a remark that "We know we can count on you to be a team player"; or something said over cocktails about "everybody does it." It is as innocent as an invitation to lunch, but it ends with loss of self, your seduction into imperial enslavement.

If you don't know who owns you, you are no match for the dominant ideology of "go along to get along."

This old story about Daniel invites you to imagine yourself afresh, to engage the powers with playful disrespect, to dare to dream, and thereby resist. The story glorifies youthful insubordination, and begs you not to surrender your dream.

(I am indebted to Walter Brueggemann, *Finally Comes the Poet: Daring Speech for Proclamation* [Minneapolis: Fortress Press, 1989], pp. 113-25, for the idea of this interpretation of the Daniel narrative.)

3

A Lamp Shining in a Dark Place

You will do well to be attentive to this as to a lamp shining in a dark place. . . . No prophecy of scripture is a matter of one's own interpretation . . . but men and women moved by the Holy Spirit spoke from God.

II Peter 1:19*b*, 20*b*-21*b*

Read II Peter 1:19-21.

YOU'RE ON YOUR WAY out into the world. How do you find your way? Christians find their way with the help of the Bible. For us, the Bible is not a rulebook, telling us exactly what to do in every situation, nor a roadmap, telling us every step to take. Rather, as is often said, the Bible is a compass, pointing us in the right direction. The Bible is a lamp, shining in an often dark and confusing world.

Christians and Buddhists differ, to a great extent, because we have listened to different stories, different depictions of the way the world is put together. A claim is being made, every Sunday, that this Bible, this book and its stories, is the key, the lens for looking at the world, the light. In the beginning was the Word (John 1); God spoke (Gen. 1) and said, "Let there be light," and there was light. Forget your physics—light is a product of speech, the word. God speaks, there is light—enlightenment. We are able to find our way only because God speaks.

"You will do well to be attentive to this as to a lamp shining in a dark place."

You have objections? The Bible is a lamp hidden under a bushel basket (Matt. 5:15). You say the Bible is often violent, narrow, primitive, incomprehensible, disordered, even weird! I say, so are you. Perhaps, with the Bible, we have at last come to the point where we can shed our modern arrogance—which has engendered such a narrow, limited view of the world, such a parochial vision of what is and what isn't—and can venture forth with a postmodern appreciation for what Karl Barth calls the "strange new world of the Bible."

The nerve of modern people to adopt a superior attitude toward the Bible! We say that the Bible is "sexist," "patriarchal," as if we weren't, as if we moderns have risen above the Bible. It is easier to see the Bible's culturally conditioned blinders than our own. The nerve of a people who have lived through surely the most bloody century of history, quibbling over a few Babylonian babies in Psalm 137!

When I was in seminary, somebody told me that my job as a preacher was to "stand in the pulpit, with the Bible in one hand and today's newspaper in the other." My job was to take this old, culturally conditioned, racist, sexist, narrow Bible, and relate it to the wonderful new modern world—and to do so in under twenty minutes. Have you noticed that the traffic all moved in the same direction on that interpretive bridge? It was always the modern world rummaging about in the Bible, telling it what was possible, what was interesting, what was permissible. If the Bible collides with our modern prejudices, our prior images of ourselves, then so much the worse for the Bible.

I've now decided that my toughest job as a preacher is not to make the Bible comprehensible to modern people, but to render modern people worthy of hearing the Bible. And that's not easy. We are parochial, myopic folk, and our vision extends no farther than that which has happened personally to us. The Bible therefore has rough going among us, not because we are sophisticated, critical, and astute, whereas the Bible is primitive, but rather because we are so contentedly naive, narrow-minded, dishonest, and inexperienced that scripture just naturally strikes us as odd.

Every time we Christians open the Bible, we play a peculiar kind of language game, and the first rule is to assume that the Bible knows more than we do. Allow me to list for you two—just two—of the Bible's most appealing characteristics as I have experienced them.

1. *The Bible is about God.* The Bible is large. But then, so is God. I don't mean that it has 1,237 pages—no, that's 1,662 pages (name another book that starts over again with page 1 after page 1237!). I mean that it is large, in that it is expansive, not easily defined or contained. It is tough for me as a preacher to say to you, without flinching, "God says," because you know that I'm human, and it's unlikely that God has a southern accent. It's just as difficult to say, when reading in Matthew, "The Bible says," because the minute you do, somebody comes along with a verse in Malachi that says just the opposite. Shake-

speare was right: "Even the devil quotes scripture for his own purposes." The Bible is about big, whereas most of us are about small. That is, most of us are desperate for a world we can measure out in a teaspoon, encapsulate into "Four Spiritual Laws," fully express on a bumper sticker, figure out over a weekend.

We think that our problem with the Bible is that it is old and primitive, whereas we are very modern. But our main problem with the Bible is that we come to church, as we do to most anywhere else, to get a better glimpse of ourselves, to receive help with ourselves, to continue the only trip modern people take—that is, deeper and deeper into our own egos. But the Bible is almost everywhere, first about God, and only secondarily, or derivatively, about us. We come to church thinking that our problem is how to be better boys and girls in the dorm next week, only to be assaulted by the Bible, which asserts that our problem is not that we are strangers to ourselves, which we are, but that we are estranged from God. The Bible longs to provoke that meeting with a true, living, big God.

2. *The Bible is about us.* The Bible is messy. Of course, so is life. Few Bible books follow neatly after one another. Stuff is repeated, for emphasis. Things are brought up, but not explained. Jesus tells stories that don't have suitable endings. In fact, the whole Bible doesn't have an ending. It just keeps going with no conclusion, with no sure statement of how things will turn out between us and God, as if to mean that the story has no ending, as if you and I are still living the story. "To be continued," is the last word of every Bible story.

And that's one reason we love the Bible. We have a hunch that it's *our* story. When we read about David, we think of ourselves at age forty-five. We read of the drunkenness and debauchery of the Philistines, and we think of Friday on campus. We hear how God came to lowly Mary, living anonymously in some backwater town, and women in our town look up.

Alas, the modern world has taught you to step back from the Bible, examine it, raise questions about it, dissect it like a cadaver, rummage about in it, in the hope of finding something with which you can agree. The Enlightenment has taught you to read in that way, and it is deadly.

My colleague, Rick Lischer, notes that the African American church, having missed the European Enlightenment, reads its Bible by stepping *into* the text, identifying with the hopeful, suffering, sinful, saved people there. So they sing, "Were you there when they crucified my Lord?" We ought, in our listening to and study of the Bible, to step courageously into the text.

The rabbis say that God, having been angered by sloppy reporting and editorial second guessing, to say nothing of what he had suffered at the hands of college professors of religion, hired a human as a secretary and began to dictate his story. It is well known that although God loves to talk, God hates to write! For forty days and nights, the secretary took dictation. Finally, the last word having been spoken, God sat down (you see, the whole time he was dictating, God was pacing about). The secretary finished the last word and stood up, threw down his pen, and with the outrage of someone who has been plagiarized, screamed, "Wait a minute, this is *my* story!"

(This legend found in John Shea, *Stories of God: An Unauthorized Biography* [Chicago: The Thomas More Press, 1978], p. 63)

4

Managing Our Miracles

"I will do this: I will pull down my barns and build larger ones, and there I will store all my grain and my goods. And I will say to my soul, 'Soul, you have ample goods laid up for many years; relax, eat, drink, be merry.'"

But God said to him, "You fool! This very night your life is being demanded of you. And the things you have prepared, whose will they be?"

Luke 12:18-20

Read Luke 12:13-21.

YOU LOOK AT YOUR DIPLOMA—that piece of paper for which you have given so many years of your life, so many tuition payments—and you are proud. That diploma is your ticket, your reassurance of prosperity and success. Considering all the hurdles you have overcome during your student years, all the exams and tests and trials, it's sort of miraculous that you have this diploma. You look at your diploma and say to yourself, "Soul, you have ample goods laid up for many years; relax, eat, drink, be merry."

This parable begins, not in contentment but in quandary. A rich man has a problem. He is the beneficiary of a spectacular harvest, a harvest so great that he has nowhere to store all of the grain.

Jesus said, "He thought to himself, 'What should I do, for I have no place to store my crops?'"

But he doesn't just build new barns to augment his old ones; he tears his old barns down and builds new barns. If he has made enough from this harvest to be tearing down old barns and building new ones, his harvest must be nothing short of miraculous. He hasn't just done well; he has done *very* well—miraculously well!

"And I will say to my soul [note that when you're this spectacularly successful, you don't need to consult anybody else—all conversation is monologue], 'Soul, you have ample goods laid up for many years; relax, eat, drink, be merry.'"

I know this story. Do you?

"Number three in your class? Wow. Take off the summer after college and have a good time. You've earned it."

"Yes, we have two who really have done very well—one in law school, one just finished med school. We really are very proud of them." Soul, you have been an A+ parent. Relax, eat, drink, be merry.

I have a job, a good job, if I do say so. And my marriage is reasonably stable, and my kids are good, never been in trouble. Soul, you have ample goods laid up for many years; relax, eat, drink, be merry.

And all this stuff—the diploma on the wall, the monthly computer printout of my retirement account, the pictures of the chaste and obedient kids on the wall, the two cars, the garage door with electronic opener—is such a comfort. It means not only that we have done a good job of the job of life, but also that we have constructed a kind of fence around life—full barns, a fat retirement account, a 3.5 GPA, a diploma on the wall—all as insurance against life's vicissitudes. Thus we are able contentedly to say, "Soul, you have ample goods laid up for many years; relax, eat, drink, be merry."

We call this the parable of the rich fool, but Jesus doesn't. Jesus begins the story not with the man, but with the land and its bounty: "The land of a rich man produced abundantly." What first impresses Jesus is this miraculous, barn-bursting harvest—a gift.

But the blessing is a burden. The land's bountiful gift becomes a big problem. And then the story becomes, How do I manage my miracle? "What should *I* do? *I* have no place to store *my* crops. *I* will do this. *I* will pull down *my* barns. *I* will store *my* grain and *my* goods. *I* will say to *my* soul, 'Relax, you have ample goods laid up for many years, eat, drink, be merry.'"

How do *I* manage *my* miracle? How do *I* supervise *my* success? It's a story about that.

As a professor, I have seen it at commencement. There are graduates who say, in one way or another, "Look at me! *I* did it!"

There are others who say, "Thanks, Mom."

As a pastor, I have seen it in the way people give to the church. There never was a correlation between a person's level of income and how much that person gave to the work of the church—at least not in churches where I was pastor. No, the giving is related to something other than income. It has to do with gratitude, a sense that what I have is not what I earned or deserved, but rather is a gift, a trust from God. That's my theory for the reason some people are givers and some are takers. It has to do with the way they manage the miracle.

We have givers and takers at universities. Only a small portion of a student's education at any school is paid for in tuition. Most of the cost of education is paid for by strangers, people we will never know, benefactors from the past. Alumni could give generously every year to the annual fund and never, in a lifetime of giving, come close to what was spent on them while they were at the university.

During a Martin Luther King, Jr., observance a few years ago, one of the speakers said, "If you are black, and if you have a good job and a secure family, you owe a fortune to the NAACP. When are you going to pay up?" Much the same can be said, in one way or another, to all of us—coaches, teachers, doctors, nurses, janitors, pastors, people whose names we will never remember. Why is it—as we sit contentedly and gaze with pride on the achievements, the accomplishments, the acquisitions of our lives—all I, my, me, mine?

A psychologist was telling me of his research relating to our self-image. He gave people some sort of test to solve, and then, when they failed to solve it or when they succeeded, he asked them to account for their failure or success. Does it surprise you to learn that he concluded with this: "We tend to blame others for our failures and to give ourselves credit for our successes"?

All the talk in this story, thus far, has been the monologue of the rich farmer. He talks to himself, plans for himself, congratulates himself, celebrates himself. I manage by my and me. It is only at the end that another voice intrudes into the story—the voice of God.

The voice does not accuse the rich man of injustice, immorality, or even greed. God calls him, "You fool!"

The man we might call prudent, far-sighted, God calls a fool. Why? He didn't get what he had unjustly. He didn't steal. Why did God call him a fool?

"You fool! This very night your life is being demanded of you. And the things you have prepared, whose will they be?" End of story.

A friend of mine pointed out that, actually, in the Greek, the line says, "Fool, this very night they shall demand your life." They? Who is this "they"? I think "they" are *the things.* The story closes with the question, "And whose will they [the things] be?" He thought the things were his problem, his opportunity, his insurance to manage as he pleased. Surprise! He belonged to the things, to manage as *they* pleased. Can we not understand the irony of a man who thought *he* had so many things, only to discover, too late, that his things had him?

We thought we were managing our modern lives with all our gadgets and things, only to discover that the things were managing us. A PBS series on the dilemmas, the horrors, the by-products of modern medicine, was titled "Managing Our Miracles." We thought we had these things. Surprise! They have us!

It's all monologue, as we pat ourselves on the back for our great material progress, our medical miracles, our great work as A+ students, our jobs, our health, our lives. And just when we get it all fenced in, hedged well about, insured, locked in, there comes that voice from the outside, that intrusive voice of God—that is, reality: "But God said to him, 'You fool! This very night they shall demand your life of you. And the things you have prepared, whose will they be?'"

This move from a self-satisfied, fat, contented, self-congratulatory monologue to the dark, intrusive, realistic, address by God is somber, but real.

Please note that God doesn't punish anyone here—unless reality be considered punishment enough. The intruding voice of God states only the facts: "Fool. This night they demand your life of you." And all that management and preparation, these big barns and prudent insurance, whose will they be?

And once again (how many times has this happened when you're reading the Bible?) the voice intrudes into my false security, my smug contentment. I am addressed. Called "fool" by the One who is the source of all that I am and all that I have.

(I am indebted to Bernard Brandon Scott, *Hear Then the Parable* [Philadelphia: Fortress Press, 1989], pp. 127-40, for the idea of this interpretation of the parable.)

5

When Through Fiery Trials

"If our God whom we serve is able to deliver us from the furnace of blazing fire and out of your hand, O king, let him deliver us. But if not . . . we will not serve your gods."

Daniel 3:17-18

Read Daniel 3:1-23, 26-28.

I WONDER IF I should tell a story like this to a sophisticated college graduate like you. The story is naive, childlike. And you are mature, analytical, sophisticated, realistic. But if you can't remember any other Bible stories from your childhood, you probably remember this one.

Sometimes, when we are all grown up and sophisticated, we return to the stories of our childhood and find that they speak in ways that are fresh and challenging. The fairy-tale reality we had been talked out of as adults may indeed be more real than what we have settled for.

King Nebuchadnezzar has a great idea for unifying his empire. A golden statue is placed at Dura. Then he sends for all the "satraps, the prefects, and the governors, the counselors, the treasurers, the justices, the magistrates" (3:2). These toadies come running breathlessly, eager to do whatever the king asks. Then he tells all these people that they must worship this golden statue whenever they "hear the sound of the horn, pipe, lyre, trigon, harp, drum, and entire musical ensemble" (3:5). Whenever they hear this musical ruckus, they are to fall to their cowardly little bureaucratic knees or "immediately be thrown into a furnace of blazing fire" (3:6). And all the satraps, prefects, governors, counselors, and clerks at the Department of Motor Vehicles, Generals at the Pentagon, and the staff of the Registrar's and Bursar's offices (you supply your own list) are only too glad to fulfill the king's wishes.

See? You thought that only a minority of our population goes to worship anymore. Think again. People who work for the government, people with titles and positions love to worship, to bow down, to fall to their knees. The horns, pipes, trigons, and drums are making a great fuss, and all these satraps, prefects, governors, and counselors are having a wonderful time, bowing before the golden statue. Everyone is getting into the act—except for three young Jews.

A delegation of toadies and sycophants comes in bowing, scraping, their knees rubbed raw with their obeisance: "O king, live forever! You have made a decree, have you not, that whenever we hear the horn, pipe, lyre, trigon, harp, and . . ."

"Yes, I know, it's my order, get on with it."

"That whenever we hear this on the PA system, we are to fall down and worship, or be thrown into a furnace of blazing fire."

"Yes, I know, and everyone seems to be having a wonderful time at the rally in support of the administration. Now nobody has time to stir up rebellion. It's made everyone proud to be a Babylonian again."

"Well, not everybody, O king, live forever!"

"What?"

"There are certain Jews who refuse to get with the program: Shadrach, Meshach, and Abednego. You promoted them, made them officials in your court, even though they are Jewish. One might think they would be grateful, but no, when there is the sound of the horn, the pipe, lyre, trigon and . . ."

"O shut up! And bring these uppity Jews to me."

Shadrach, Meshach, and Abednego (what great names!) are brought before the king.

"Didn't I make it perfectly clear that whenever you people hear the horn, the pipe, lyre, and so on, that you are supposed to hit the dirt and worship my nice statue?"

Shadrach was about 22 years of age, Meshach was nearly 24, and Abednego was about the same. You can tell they're about that age, because they have so little respect for authority!

"O Nebuchadnezzar," [note the contrast between the way those bootlicking toadies talked to the king and the way these upstarts talk] "we have no need to present a defense to you in this matter. If our God whom we serve is able to deliver us from the furnace of blazing fire and out of your hand, O king, let him deliver us. But if not, be it known to you, O king, that we will not serve your gods" (3:16-18*a*).

Nebuchadnezzar went berserk. He not only ordered that Shadrach, Meshach, and Abednego be thrown into the furnace, he ordered that the furnace be made seven times hotter than usual. Then he peered into the fiery furnace, and behold, he saw these three walking around inside the furnace, and a fourth! The young men had been joined by a fourth figure, shadowy, unknown, strolling with them in the furnace.

Nebuchadnezzar was amazed. It had been a long time since there was anybody around who had disobeyed, or even questioned one of his royal decrees, particularly in the name of religion. Nebuchadnezzar said, "Your God must be some god!"

And they lived happily ever after, until their next confrontation with the government.

Now, I know that part of you thinks you are above a childlike, playful story like this one. We are conditioned to believe that these Bible stories are too good to be true, products of an overwrought imagination. We think this way because we are more familiar with stories of threatened, oppressed young women and men, which end quite differently. Most of the stories of political oppression that we have learned about do not end with the condemned dancing in the furnace, the king converted, and those who were condemned being given freedom and a promotion.

Our stories tell of a group of Haitian schoolgirls who chanted the name of ousted Aristide on their school ground, and were gunned down by the Haitian military. No God entered the fiery furnace for them.

So what if this story of the three young men had ended differently? What if three Jews dared to question the royal edict and were incinerated? But you already know *that* story. A crowd of Jews was huddled in the so-called camp shower, and the guard (just following orders!) poured cyanide through the ceiling, and in a few horrible, gasping moments, it was over. No divine intervention. No fourth figure walking with them into the gas chamber. You know *that* story.

The story of Shadrach, Meshach, and Abednego could have ended that way. Such stories usually end that way. What then?

The three young men give answer: "If our God whom we serve is able to deliver us from the furnace of blazing fire and out of your hand, O king, let him deliver us. But if not, be it known to you, O king, that we will not serve your gods" (3:17-18*a*).

I am amazed (are you?) by the candor, the honesty of that *if*: "*If* our God whom we serve is able to deliver us." The stance of the three young men is not based on some facile theological assertion: "Our God always delivers. God is in the deliverance business, particularly for nice Hebrew boys like us. Our God *will* deliver us. No sweat." That's not what they said. They said, "*If* our God is able to deliver us." They leave deliverance in God's hands, where I suppose it is in such circumstances, if we are as honest as they.

And perhaps most surprising of all, they still serve God, still do what's right, still stand up to the king and take the consequences. "If our God is able to deliver us . . . . *But if not . . . we will not serve your gods.*"

What I thought was a little fairy tale of wishful thinking turns on me and asks where I stand with God. Why are you reading this book? What do you expect in return from God? Who among us serves God for no reward?

Oh, we may not be in a fiery furnace at the moment, but when we are, we expect to call in our markers, remind God, "Remember me? Third pew from the right, Sunday, September 3?"

Are we able to pray, with the three young men, "If God is able to deliver me from this cancer and out of the hand of evil, let God do so. But if not, be it known to all, O forces of sickness, evil, and death, I will not worship your golden idols"? "If God can answer my prayers and fix my family . . . but if not, be it known that I will worship only this God"?

Do you serve God, worship, put your money in the plate, pray, and try to do right for nothing? I'm not sure that I do, for when I am not delivered from my modest furnaces, I am apt to feel terribly betrayed, and I want to know, Why? I kept *my* part of the bargain. Why didn't God?

The story ends with great, arrogant, powerful Nebuchadnezzar overwhelmed at the courage of these three young men in the furnace. I think Nebuchadnezzar would have been filled with awe, even if the three young men had *not* been delivered, so amazed was he to find such impudent, youthful courage running free in his slave empire. This playful, exuberant story of Shadrach, Meshach, and Abednego has given life to the oppressed and the persecuted down through the ages.

To me, it offers a question: Am I able to serve God, to bow only before God's altar, expecting nothing in return? Would I be able to say before the conforming powers of this world, "If the God I serve is able to deliver me, let him deliver me. But if not, be it known that I will not serve other gods"?

6

Hints of Transcendence

Then their eyes were opened, and they recognized him; and he vanished from their sight.

Luke 24:31

Read Luke 24:13-35.

A YEAR OR SO AGO, a friend of mine died. . . . One morning in his sixty-eighth year he simply didn't wake up. . . . He died in March, and in May my wife and I were staying with his widow overnight when I had a short dream about him. I dreamed he was standing there in the dark guest room where we were asleep looking very much himself in the navy blue jersey and white slacks he often wore. I told him how much we had missed him and how glad I was to see him again. . . . Then I said, "Are you really there, Dudley." . . . His answer was that he was really there. "Can you prove it?" I asked him. "Of course," he said. Then he plucked a strand of wool out of his jersey and tossed it to me. I caught it . . . and the feel of it was so palpably real that it woke me up. . . . I told the dream at breakfast the next morning, and I'd hardly finished when my wife spoke. She said that she'd seen the strand on the carpet as she was getting dressed. . . . I rushed upstairs to

see for myself, and there it was—a little tangle of navy blue wool.
(Frederick Buechner, *The Clown in the Belfry* [New York: Harper Collins, 1992], pp. 7-8)

Thus the writer Frederick Buechner describes a moment, a wistful, intrusive moment of transcendence. Now, what was that? Coincidence? Maybe. *Maybe not.*

I was on my way to a speaking engagement in Chattanooga. And as I clung to the seat of the little airplane for reassurance, my mind slipped back to ten years ago, in the spring, when I was being hired for a job at Duke University. There was a student, a law student, who asked me, "What kind of minister do you plan to be at Duke?"

I remembered the question, though all I could remember of the student was his first name, Porter. And why was I thinking of that question, and that student now, since I had never, as far as I know, thought of it before, and it had nothing to do with the matters at hand?

The plane landed. I spoke that night. Three days after I returned home, I received a note from a lawyer who said he was in the auditorium when I spoke, but did not get to see me afterward. His name was Porter.

Now, what was that? Some sort of glitch in the brain? Coincidence? Maybe. *Maybe not.*

The odds against such occurrences must be astronomical. And yet, if we had the courage to talk about them, I expect we would find that they happen all the time. It's not interesting that such moments occur, for they certainly do, but what's interesting is what we make of them. Or refuse to make of them.

Something about us is fearful to make too much of them. I squirm as Buechner says of his dream, "Maybe my friend really did come to me in my dream . . . . Maybe it is true that by God's grace, the dead are given back their lives . . . and the doctrine of the resurrection of the body is not just a doctrine" (p. 9).

Maybe. *Maybe not.*

Maybe these moments (and I know you've had them) are coincidence. A fluke. Then maybe they are playful intrusions into our so common-sensical patterns of thought—a blue thread on the carpet, a face and a voice plucked from the past—sent by heaven to disrupt us. A peek behind the curtain of exterior reality. A whisper of transcendence. A suggestion that there is more to death than mere death, more to my past and present than a trip to Chattanooga.

Maybe we shouldn't make such a fuss over such moments. Maybe they mean nothing beyond certain glitches in the electrical throbs of the brain. Or maybe they mean everything, connect us with a reality too deep, too real, and so wonderful that, if we were to look at it face-to-face, we would be incinerated by its glory. So all we get is a peek. Hints.

I would hate to see you make too much of such moments, bet too much of your life on a blue thread or a Chattanooga lawyer's note. For behind the curtain, there may be only emptiness. The voice you think you hear may be the wind and nothing more. Of course, you are betting your life on something. Most of us live by what we can hold, touch, and chew, not on something that can be dismissed as mere coincidence.

The lives derived thereby may be flat, but at least they are unequivocal. And having bet our lives on the comfortingly unambiguous, something about us is annoyed—yes, annoyed, when the mysterious vertical intersects the sure and certain horizontal. We are annoyed that God may be a tease.

Buechner adds, "A coincidence can be . . . God's way of remaining anyonymous, or it can be just a coincidence" (p. 11). A dream may be no more than wishful thinking, or it may be a privileged peek into the inner workings of what's really going on in the world.

Maybe God really does come out to meet us, but maybe it's always on God's terms, not ours. Maybe God flirts, loves to tease us toward a reality that we—with our facts and figures, empiricism and suburban common sense—routinely walk past without a twitch of curiosity. Maybe we're all like the kid who wore earphones so long with volume turned all the way up, that the heavy metal music rendered his eardrums impervious to Debussy or a whisper.

Maybe we don't see God much because we've lost the capacity to look. So messages slipped to us from the other side are reflexively dismissed as "coincidence," and a divine voice is heard only as a consequence of indigestion.

The Chair of our Chemistry Department told me that the best research chemist he knew was a man who got out of bed every morning, looked out his bedroom window, and said aloud, "What is going on out there today?" So maybe the trouble with contemporary chemists is that they think they already know something. They go to the lab without expectation of shock or surprise. Science dies without imagination.

Sometimes, something is there, but we can't see it. Our eyes are dulled, or our vision is unformed, undisciplined to look with appropriate curiosity and intelligence. If what's there is God, we shouldn't expect to see it too clearly, because God is large, thick, ambiguous, if God be God.

It was Sunday, and two disciples were walking from Jerusalem to the little village of Emmaus, trying to make sense of the horrible events of the past three days. Jesus was dead.

It was a good campaign while it lasted, but they didn't get him elected Messiah. He was dead. It's over. Finished.

And they became aware of this stranger, walking beside them, on the way.

"What were you talking about?" he inquired. "You look depressed."

"Are you the only person in Jerusalem who hasn't read the papers?" they asked.

"What's happpened?"

"Jesus of Nazareth, a wonderful prophet, how they handed him over to death, killed him. We had hoped . . . but . . . . Some of our women came back from the cemetery with some fiction about his body not being in the tomb, and some vision, grief reaction, concidence, post-traumatic stress syndrome, wishful thinking, feminine hysteria."

And beginning with Genesis, working all the way back through Revelation, the stranger "opened the scriptures" for them, explained it all to them. And, true to form, the disciples understand . . . nothing. Now, why couldn't they see?

When they arrived at Emmaus, as the sun was setting, they bid the stranger to break bread with them. Then there, at table, the stranger took the bread, broke the bread, gave the bread, and their eyes were opened. They saw.

And they ran all the way back to Jerusalem to tell the others about the moment, the breaking of the bread at the table, the way the curtain had been drawn back for a stunning glimpse.

And some even believed. But the majority of those polled said it had to be some kind of a coincidence. Male hysteria.

Maybe. *Maybe not!*

7

Take Heart

They were terrified . . . they cried out in fear. But immediately Jesus spoke to them and said, "Take heart, it is I; do not be afraid."

Matthew 14:26*b*, *c*-27

Read Matthew 14:22-33.

LIFE MAY BE SMOOTH sailing for you right now, as you graduate from college and begin your adult life. But no matter how well things may be going for you now, you will not always sail on smooth seas. What then?

Jesus commands his disciples to get in a boat and move out onto the sea. He *makes* them get into the boat. Maybe they want to stay at home on the reassuring land. No, he makes them move out.

As for Jesus, he goes away by himself, seeking time alone. At this point in Matthew's Gospel, opposition to Jesus is growing. Increasingly, he is isolated because of his teaching and his work. Now he seeks to be alone to pray, sending his disciples on ahead of him. And "he was there alone."

And what would he have prayed? As a faithful Jew, surely he prayed the *Shema*, the prayer of Israel: "Hear O Israel, the Lord your God is *one*." Jesus, increasingly isolated, prays the prayer of God's absolute oneness, uniqueness, aloneness. God is one. At evening, Jesus is there alone. And we, aware of what lies ahead, know that he is alone not only geographically, but personally. At evening, he is alone.

The disciples, out in the boat, are soon "far from land"—literally, "many *stadia* at a distance." One of these *stadia* is 200 yards. There is a great distance between Jesus and his disciples. He is alone with God in prayer; they are alone in the boat on the sea.

The boat is buffeted by the waves, thrashed and battered. The word in Greek here is *bazanidzomenon*. You can almost feel the battering waves in the word itself, can't you? Say it. *Bazanidzomenon*. Boom. Boom.

"By the waves and the wind," the boat is buffeted. What do you think of when you hear "waves and wind"? Do you hear echoes of Genesis 1? The Spirit of God, the "wind" moved over the face of the waters. There is an echo, just a little reminiscence of this creative wind.

Our remembrance of creation is confirmed when we are told what time it is. This text in Matthew says just "early in the morning," but in the Greek, it's "at the fourth watch." The fourth watch is from three to six o'clock in the morning, at the very break of day. Here at the beginning of a new day, some time just before dawn, the little boat of the disciples is being battered by the waves and the wind, and here comes Jesus, walking on the waters, coming toward them.

Look! "It is a ghost!" they cry. It's a *phantazma*. They're afraid of the waves, the wind, but they're also afraid of this approaching form. Is this a ghost? Who is this?

"Take heart, it is I; do not be afraid," Jesus says. He says to them, "It is I." In the Greek, this is *ego eimi*—literally, "I am."

Is that an echo of some other scripture in your mind? "Take courage, I am. I am."

Back in the book of Exodus, the Exodos out of Egyptian slavery begins—the dawning of the new day—as Moses stands before the burning bush and a voice says, "I am." In this rather amazing moment here on the lake, the disciples hear a deep voice saying, "I am."

Peter blurts out, "If it is you, command me to come to you on the water."

And Peter launches out "on the water." And again we hear an echo back to Genesis 1, when the Spirit moved over the face of the waters and created a new world out of chaos.

Then we are told that when Peter felt the strong wind, he cried, "Save me!" The waters were up to his neck!

Maybe he was in Missouri beside the rising river, or in the hospital talking to an oncologist, or up in the front office talking to the boss, when he prayed, "Save me!"

Jesus reached out his hand to Peter and called to him, "You of little faith, why did you doubt?" This is a constant theme throughout the Gospel of Matthew: doubt. Why do we doubt? These disciples are not perfect; they are like us. They doubt when they feel the wind, see the waves, water up to the neck. They begin to sink. But Jesus keeps working with them.

Finally, by the end of Matthew's Gospel, Jesus gathers his disciples on a mountain, appears before them in all his glory, telling them to go into all the world, telling them, "I am with you always." At that moment, they fall to their knees and worship him. However, even then, Matthew says, "Some doubted."

Right down to the end, to the very last chapter of the Gospel, some doubted. They struggle with it, they try to figure out who he is and what he is doing with them. And though some doubt, Jesus keeps struggling with them, keeps reaching out. Their doubt is all right, because God is with them, reaching out to them.

As a child, I remember being sent down our winding drive that made its way out through the woods to the highway—sent out at night to retrieve something from the mailbox. It was dark. There were no streetlights, nothing out there but dark, threatening woods. I hated that trip, especially at night, when you never knew what might jump at you, and nobody could hear you cry out.

Once as I made my way, nearing the road, I heard footsteps! Footsteps coming toward me. What could I do? Try to make it back to the house? Such heavy footsteps surely could catch me before I made it to safety. My heart beat faster. The footsteps came closer. I was about to cry out, "Save me!" when a familiar voice from the darkness called, "it's Uncle Charles."

Don't be afraid. It is I. Just a voice, that's all. The words: It is I. Jesus reaches out to us. A world is transformed; we are saved.

As he got into the boat with them, they bowed down and worshiped, saying, "Truly you *are* the Son of God."

When Mark tells this story in his Gospel, all the disciples can say at the end is, "Who is this?" In Mark, they don't get it. Their hearts are hardened.

In Matthew, it's different. In this stunning moment, Jesus is identified by his disciples as the Son of God, God's right hand. We are conditioned, by our modern minds, to ask *how*. Rather, the disciples ask *who?* We ask *how* could Jesus be both fully human and fully God? We ask *how* could he have stilled the waves? The disciples are instructing us to ask *who*. Who is this, that even the wind and the seas obey? Here, caught in the boat, buffeted by wind and waves, at night, just before dawn, they know.

Peter, the one Jesus nicknamed "Little Faith," is saved by allowing Jesus to reach out to him, to grasp him by the hand. Fortunately, it doesn't take much faith; even as little as a mustard seed will do (Matthew 13).

Peter ventured forth on nothing more than the gut-level recognition that it was nearly dawn. Faith is not some closed-eyed, teeth-clenched determination to believe the inconceivable. Faith is venturing forth on the waters, tossed by wind and waves, in the conviction that a new day, a new world is 'a comin'. Rather than taking out insurance, feathering our nest, perfecting pension plans, we venture forth in faith, out on the waves with God.

Jesus made his disciples go on ahead of him in the boat, alone out on the sea. Yet when things didn't work out, when they were *bazanidzomenon*ed by the waves, he came to them, reached out to them, saved them, and they saw that the Son of God was with them. It was dawn.

Little faith is enlarged by daring to venture forth in the middle of the storm. Faithful discipleship sometimes means the willingness to let Jesus put us in the boat and launch us out onto some unknown sea. (He *made* them get in the boat.) It is only as we test the waters that we experience the voice ("Take heart. It is I.") and his strong right hand.

It's the dawn of a new day. Take heart.

(Thanks to Dr. William Mallard for exegetical insights in his Bible studies at Lake Junaluska during the 1993 Ministers Conference.)

8

Just an Old-fashioned Love Song

"Arise, my love, my fair one,
and come away;
for now the winter is past,
the rain is over and gone.
The flowers appear on the earth;
the time of singing has come."
Song of Solomon 2:10*b*-12*a*

Read Song of Solomon 2:8-13.

IF YOU HAVE BEEN so unfortunate as to not yet experience it firsthand, these are the words of two people in love, sixth-century B.C. style. People about your age have a notorious habit of falling in love, as these two lovers did. Does it surprise you that the words of these lovers have made it into Holy Scripture? This unabashed Hebrew love poem, the Song of Solomon, is one of only two books in the Bible never to mention the word *God.* Preachers down through the ages have puzzled themselves over this poetry. Give us clergy a rule, a law, some noble platitude or grim admonition, and we're off to the races. Give us a languid summer afternoon, two young people on a blanket in the park, and we get nervous.

> My beloved is like a gazelle
>   or a young stag.
> Look, there he stands. . . .
> The fig tree puts forth its figs,
>   and the vines are in blossom.

It's about love—exuberant, pointless, wonderful love. Not the clean, holy *agape* of Christians and the church, but the messy, entangling *eros* of Hollywood and sixteen-year-olds—and some eighty-year-olds!

Love, in its early stages, is an intense state that displays some familiar features: being consumed with thoughts of the other person; wanting to be together constantly; losing sleep; resorting to poetry, even when one is not a poet; deliciously wasting hours gazing across a table during candlelight dinners. Behavior of this sort is an outward and visible sign of an inward and spiritual dislocation called *love*, or, more accurately at this early stage, *infatuation*, which to those in love seems perfectly acceptable, but seems crazy to everyone who is not.

Now if this initial period of infatuation continues, it will sometimes, but not always, transmute itself into something called romantic love—or else it will eventually disappear, thereafter to be regretted long afterward, when we look back on this period of our lives and say, "I can't believe what a fool I made of myself."

Love is a term for that time when two people will feel that they have united to form a new entity in the world called a *we* (see Robert Solomon, *Love* [Garden City, N.Y.:

Anchor Books, 1981]). Harvard philosopher Robert Nozick says that "the desire to form a 'we' is intrinsic to the nature of love" (*The Examined Life* [New York: Simon & Schuster, 1989], p. 70). Love is about the gracious movement from the "I" to the "we" (a movement which feels something like falling from a very great height into a pool of gelatin).

When you're in love with someone, your whole being is tied up with that person. You care about what that person cares about, want to be where that person is. We call people who have formed this *we* a *couple.* Moreover, they feel like a couple, think and act like a couple; that is, they have a new, distinct, more complex identity than that which was formerly just "I" or merely "me." Surely this is what Jesus had in mind when he spoke, referring to Genesis 1, of the two becoming one flesh in marriage. Note that most of the action in the Song of Songs is consumed with getting ready to be with the beloved, thrilling at being with the beloved, and then claiming to be near death when absent from the beloved. *I've* got to be *we.*

I also think that this explains why so many lovers cling to the implausible notion that their beloved is the one and only right person in the world for them. That is a thought, I think, that comes *after* their "we" has been formed, after that time when they are so naturally one. This other has become such a natural, comfortable part of who they are, has released so many wonderful aspects of their personality, that they naturally find it inconceivable that life could be otherwise than with this one particular person. This other has become so successfully part of the "we" that the other seems hardly other at all. It all seems so right that it is virtually impossible to convince lovers that God did not reach down from heaven to pair them just this way.

A word of caution (which is always the last sort of word lovers are able to hear): Even though there is now, by love, this "we," it need not mean, indeed must not mean, the dissolution of the "I." When you're in love with another, you are in love with the other—not the other merged into the "me," but the *other*, with all his or her delightful particularities and oddities. If the "we" were to consume the other, there would be no one there to love; so the other must retain a sense of being another, in all his or her quirkiness.

People want to be loved, as they say, "for themselves," as they are, rather than as a reforming spouse someday might make them. We therefore love "Jack," or we are crazy about "Jill," with a face, a name. Which is one reason the Song of Songs goes on and on, taking to rather ridiculous limits poetic descriptions of feet, breasts, neck, toes, fingers compared to gazelles, palm trees, figs, and various kinds of fruit. You, to the lover, are so exactly, so uniquely, so lovably . . . *you.* Every inch of you (and by the time the Song ends, we have covered about every inch!).

Jesus' talk of two becoming one flesh was his way of pointing to the mystery of how two—so particular, so unique (all the more beloved for their particularities, down to the feet, neck, and toes)—can feel so much like "we." When the formerly just "me" becomes part of the loving "we," it is almost as if there is another, a better "me."

It's no wonder that romantic love quickly finds sex as a vehicle of its expression. Love longs to reproduce itself, to populate the whole world with little carbon copies of the beloved. Nothing is more generous than love in wanting to share itself, nor is anything any greedier in wanting everything—toes, neck, arms, everything—all the way.

The mention of sex reminds me: Nothing is more wonderful, nor much more dangerous than love. We are never more wonderful and self-giving than when we are in love—and never more self-deceitful. I wish I knew how to sort out all of this, that I had guidelines to offer for when it's "really" love and when it is only a consuming, self-aggrandizing infatuation, but I don't. All I can say is that the church, having a healthy respect for the ambiguous, morally dangerous aspects of our declarations of love, has found it helpful to test those intimate declarations with more public promises of lifetime commitment: marriage.

When we're in love, we're not in love with humanity in general. As the Song of Solomon demonstrates, what we love is the tiny idiosyncracies—his cute little twists of mind concerning inconsequential matters like the way to squeeze a tube of toothpaste; the way she stirs her coffee.

There is almost nothing more gracious that you can do for another person than to love that person. To expose yourself to the gaze of another, to risk being seen by that person as your true self, to let your lives get all mixed up together. There isn't much more one can give another than that.

Perhaps that's why we're notorious for avoiding romance like the plague, knowing in our heart of hearts how much it costs, how risky such entanglements are to our much-cherished autonomy. This is at least one reason monogamy is invariably linked to romantic love, for we cannot bear the thought of anyone else having access to so unique, so intensely particular and intimate a relationship as that in which we have thrown caution to the wind and so thoroughly enjoyed losing ourselves.

And I'm fighting the tendency to claim that any of this will do you good. Note that the Song of Solomon has, as far as we can tell, absolutely no edifying intent, no moral, no thought for the day or helpful hints for homemakers. Love tends to be utterly nonpragmatic, nonfunctional. For a lover to ask the beloved, "What have you done for me lately?" is to demonstrate grim utilitarianism, not love. To ask of lovers engaged in a kiss, "Now what good does that do?" shows a stupidity about love so deep as to be pathetic.

So there isn't much here to help you make it through the week, or to help you in your next job interview, or to strengthen you in your struggles as a Christian disciple. This is simply an old-fashioned love song, an invitation to enjoy God's gift of romance.

Ah, see them there, locked in sweet, expectant embrace for all eternity, enjoying the union of the lonely "I" into the strengthened "we," quivering at the thought of a mere sight of the beloved. She speaks:

> Look, he comes,
> . . . like a gazelle or a young stag.

He exclaims:

> Arise, my love, my fair one,
>   and come away;
> for now the winter is past,
>   the rain is over and gone.
> The flowers appear on the earth;
>   the time of singing has come.

9

Returning

"In the wilderness prepare the way of the LORD,
make straight in the desert a highway for our God.
Every valley shall be lifted up,
and every mountain and hill be made low;"
. . . "Here is your God!"

Isaiah 40:3-4*a*, 9*d*

Read Isaiah 40:1-11.

BEGINNING IN THE SUMMER after my college graduation, I got lost," she said.

"Lost?" I asked.

"Yep. When I was in school, I had a goal, some direction. Then, when I graduated, I realized that I didn't know how to do anything except go to school. So I just wandered here and there for a couple of years. Lost. Then I returned home."

Do you know what it is to be lost? Do you know what it means to return home?

The people of Israel are in exile, captive in Babylon. Into this exilic gloom, Isaiah the prophet speaks:

> Comfort, O comfort my people,
> says your God. . . .
> "In the wilderness prepare the way of the LORD,
> make straight in the desert a highway for our God.
> Every valley shall be lifted up,
> and every mountain and hill be made low."

It's the announcement of a divine highway construction program through the wilderness, the lostness, from Babylonian exile back home. Note that it's a straight road. Ordinarily, the way back from Babylonia to Israel followed the Fertile Crescent, going out of the way to avoid the desert wilderness. But this road is "straight in the desert." Note that it is the Lord who will be traveling that road, leading Israel homeward. It's the announcement of homecoming.

The last church I served as pastor was next to a synagogue. The rabbi and I had coffee together on Mondays. I was telling the rabbi about our new ministry to single young adults. Always the most difficult age group to reach, suddenly young adults were coming back to church. I had asked a group of them what they would like most from the church. They responded, "Organize a Bible study group for us. We want to know the Bible."

I told them to name a teacher, and I would get him or her to lead the group. "We want Van Watson," they said, naming a nearly seventy-year-old retired schoolteacher. I got Van, and the group was off to a great start.

"What's going on?" I asked the rabbi. "These young adults coming back to church. Is anything like this happening in the synagogue?"

"Sure," he said. "Hardly a week goes by that somebody in their mid-twenties doesn't show up saying, 'I want to be a Jew again. My folks hardly ever went to synagogue. I want to come back.' "

"What is this?" I wondered.

"They're looking for their parents," replied the rabbi. "They've been raised by a generation so uncertain of its own values that it didn't dare pass them on to their young. They're looking for roots. They're looking for parents." They're looking for home.

> "In the wilderness prepare the way of the LORD,
> make straight in the desert a highway for our God."

Surely Isaiah means for us to think of earlier Israel on its Exodus through the wilderness. Getting free from Pharaoh was not the toughest Exodus task. Between Egyptian slavery and freedom of the Promised Land lay wilderness. And when you hear the word "wilderness," you are not to think back-to-nature-freaks in their cozy prefab cabin in the woods, nor are you to have visions of hiking in the Adirondacks on your vacation. Wilderness, for Israel, was a place of wild beasts, temptation, sin, and bewildered wandering with no star for guidance. It took Israel forty years of wandering to finally find the way home.

I know a man who took forty years to find the way home. Dan Wakefield, in his popular book *Returning*, describes how he wandered away from God, how his life as an adult became chaotic, confused:

> I cannot pinpoint any particular time when I suddenly believed in God again. I only know that such belief came to seem as natural as for all but a few stray moments of twenty-five or more years before it had been inconceivable. I realized this while looking at fish.

> I had gone with my girl friend to the New England Aquarium, and as we gazed at the astonishingly brilliant colors of some of the small tropical fish—reds and yellows and oranges and blues . . . . I wondered how anyone could think that all this was the result of some chain of accidental explosions! Yet . . . to try to convince me otherwise five years before would have been hopeless. Was this what they called "conversion"? . . .
>
> I didn't *feel* "reborn." No voice came out of the sky nor did a thunderclap strike me . . . I was relieved when our minister explained that the literal translation of "conversion" . . . is not "rebirth" but "turning." That's what my own experience felt like—as if I'd been walking in one direction and then, in response to some inner pull, I turned.
> (New York: Penguin Books, 1988 [pp. 23-24])

> Get you up to a high mountain,
>   O Zion, herald of good tidings;
> lift up your voice with strength . . .
> say to the cities of Judah,
>   "Here is your God!"

Wilderness is a metaphor for lostness, exile, homelessness. Note the good news that this is *God's* highway. God brings homeless people back home. I teach a freshman course, "The Search for Meaning." (I talk to the students about humanity's search for a meaningful life, and they talk to me about their search for an easy A!) We enjoy thinking of ourselves as folk who search for God, people searching for answers to life's tough questions.

But note in the scripture above that no one has been searching for God. The text tells of what God will do, where God is going, dragging Israel along, down the straight road home. No one asked for John the Baptist. The way out of the wilderness is a way initiated by, led by, God. So the question is not, What am I looking for? or, What would it take for me to grope my way back home? The question is, What road is *God* building toward you today?

Those words are not spoken to you, but at some time you may hear them as if spoken only for you. That face from the past. That vaguely felt but gnawing sense of yearning. That echo evoked from deep within the soul's memory, upon hearing again a carol not heard since childhood. That coincidence that might not have been merely coincidental. I wonder.

> "In the wilderness prepare the way of the LORD,
> make straight in the desert a highway for our God."

Wilderness is that place, which is not a place, where we lose our way, wander from the path, get lost. Exile is that time when we become enslaved to false gods, serve an alien empire, sell out, forget.

Fred Craddock remembers a little girl from one of his early pastorates. Her parents sent her to church, but never came with her. They would pull in the church's circular drive, the little girl would hop out of the car, and they would go out for Sunday breakfast. The father was an executive, upwardly mobile, ambitious.

The whole town knew of their Saturday night parties, given not for entertainment, but rather as part of their whole upwardly mobile program. That determined who was invited. And the whole town knew of the wild things that went on at those parties.

But every Sunday, there was the little girl.

One Sunday, Craddock says he looked out over his congregation and thought, "There she is with a couple of adult friends." Later, he realized that she was there with her mom and dad. At the end of the service, when the invitation was given, her mom and dad came down front to join the church.

"What prompted this?" the young pastor asked later.

"Do you know about our parties?" they asked.

"Yes, I heard of them," said the pastor.

"Well, we had one last night again. It got a bit loud, and there was much drinking. The noise waked our daughter, and she came downstairs, and she was on about the third step. And she saw the eating and drinking and said, 'Oh, can I give the blessing? God is great, God is good, let us thank him for our food. Goodnight, everybody.' And she went back upstairs. People began to say, 'It's getting late, we really must be going,' and 'Thanks for a great evening,' " and within two minutes the room was empty."

Mom and dad had picked up the crumpled napkins and spilled peanuts, half-sandwiches, and empty glasses, and taken them into the kitchen. And they looked at each other, and he said what they both were thinking: "Where do we think we're going?" God had come out for them. Remembrance. Homecoming.

> "In the wilderness prepare the way of the LORD,
> make straight in the desert a highway for our God.
> Every valley shall be lifted up,
> and every mountain and hill be made low;"
> . . . "Here is your God!"

10

Left to the Lions?

"For he is the living God,
enduring forever. . . .
He delivers and rescues . . .
for he has saved Daniel
from the power of the lions."
Daniel 6:26-27

Read Daniel 6:1-27.

THIS IS A GOOD STORY. Even if you don't know many Bible stories, you may know this one about little Daniel in the lions' den.

I heard about a Sunday school teacher who showed her class a graphic picture of Christians being thrown to the lions in Roman times. She, not being too bright about the nature of five-year-olds, undoubtedly expected her charges to sympathize with these martyred Christians. But one little girl said, "Look, there's a poor lion over there who has no more Christians to eat."

We are supposed to sympathize with little Daniel, and sympathize we do. We sympathize with him not only because, as a young Jew in the court of the Babylonia king, he is in a vulnerable position, and because we always sympathize with the underdog, but also we are immediately attracted to Daniel because he is the quintessential "young person on the way up." And you are a young person on the way up, so listen up.

We are told that Daniel "distinguished himself above all the other presidents and satraps because an excellent spirit was in him" (v. 3). And we know that the scripture is speaking truthfully, because we find that his bureaucratic colleagues hate him! Mediocrity hates excellence! Nothing so disrupts the office coffee hour, or the teachers' lounge, or the company cafeteria as the discovery of some new, young, ambitious, eager, and, worst of all, *competent* young person on the way up. That's Daniel, and they hate him.

So all these bureaucratic toadies go bowing and scraping to the king, "O King Darius, live forever!" and ask for a piece of legislation to order that, just for thirty days, everyone in the kingdom must pray only to King Darius.

These petty government bureaucrats have figured out that they "shall not find any ground for complaint against this Daniel" (v. 5) *unless* it has to do with his God. They know that this is what sets Daniel apart from them. As good pagans, they are eager to worship any god, as long as it unifies the government, or makes them feel better, or pumps up their self-esteem, or gives them a religious buzz; but this Daniel, this Jew, is something else again.

Daniel's undoing is brought about by a rule—the "Law of the Medes and the Persians"—that proverbial law which can be changed by no one, not even the king. "The Law of the Medes and the Persians" is an irrevocable, fixed, no exceptions type rule, a type loved by the IRS, the college Registrar, the Bursar's office. "Sorry, no exception, period!"

Bureaucrats, people who are paid to write and administer rules, love the "Law of the Medes and the Persians" because no thought is required to administer laws of this sort. The philosopher Alasdair MacIntyre says that we are increasingly in the grip of such laws because the real high priest of our culture is the "manager," those persons without feeling, insight, or principles, people who simply find rules and apply them, managing conflicting claims without making judgment, without any goal or vision. The "Law of the Medes and Persians" is perfect for such a society.

Now we are faced with the prospect of a sympathetic but impotent king, caught in a tangle of his own rules. Odd, that this king who was alleged to be so powerful that he was like a god, has now made a rule that even he can't change. People at the very top, like King Darius, usually are sympathetic, but they often are as caught as folk on the bottom, like Daniel.

You don't like the way you've been treated by some underling in the front office, so you demand to see his boss, and the boss is always unfailingly sympathetic to your case, but unable to do anything about it. "I'd love to help you, but . . . ." "Nothing would please me more, but . . . ." High-minded, decent, trapped in a web of rules, guidelines, policies, and procedures, we talk pitifully about how free, unrestricted, and autonomous we are. Modern life has a kind of caughtness about it, despite our claims of such freedom. We have exchanged the rule of King Darius for the rule of a nameless, faceless bureaucrat. Pontius Pilate, who bore no personal ill will toward Jesus, was "just following rules." The caseworker at the welfare office waits for a form to be signed, while a family goes hungry. The engineer on the train filled with Jews headed toward the camp was not responsible for the contents of the train. It was all a kind of bureaucratic jam, the Holocaust.

Both King Darius and little Daniel are trapped. The king is absurdly, impotently trapped by his bureaucratic state and its rules. Daniel is trapped by his obedience to God rather than to human law (see Acts 5:29). And there is a great difference. How odd that the king who supposedly is completely free and sovereign is totally enslaved. Daniel, who is supposed to be a slave, is the only free person in the story.

And there's no freedom without risk. Note that nothing in the story tells us that Daniel will be spared the choice between risky obedience to God and virtually certain death at the hands of the empire. No one can protect him from this choice between good and evil.

Daniel is thus in a position known to us, forced to choose between a human law and the law of God, without guarantee of protection or success.

Now, in one of the great stories of the Bible, little Daniel goes to the lions. King Darius, trapped as much as Daniel, has a miserable night, tossing and turning. Next morning at daybreak, the king scurries to the lions' den. "Daniel, are you still there?" he calls. Miraculously, Daniel is unscathed.

Here is good news, gospel, for the obedient faithful, those who bow down before no idols and worship the true God, no matter the cost. That's good news for all the whistle-blowers, morally upright young people like you, who refuse to do "insider trading," though "everyone else does it" at the brokerage house; who refuse to sign off on shoddy workmanship, though it's commonly done in this firm; who refuse to compromise academic principle and promote this student, even though he can't read, because the principal said to. Good news! It pays to have standards, principles, to worship this God.

But the news gets even better! Next day, those who accused Daniel, all those little bureaucratic bean counters and toadies, and their wives, and their children are thrown to the lions and torn limb from limb even before they hit the ground! I told you this was a great story. And we love this story! Oh, sweet justice.

Don't tell me that you are offended by this. You love this part of the story! Down there at the bottom of the ravenous lions' den, torn limb from limb, is the woman from the Department of Motor Vehicles who denied your license because you didn't have ten dollars in cash, the registrar who wouldn't let you transfer three hours credit from your summer at UCLA. You love this story!

This story of Daniel, Darius, and the lions is not meant to be a morality tale. It's a childlike fairy tale of a story, meant to inspire childlike confidence in the justice of God, even in the darkness, even in the jaws of death, with no guarantee that the story will end well or that goodness will be vindicated. Behind the story is a question: Would *we* serve God—go against the flow, resist the rules, hold our head high before the president or the boss, refuse to compromise or cheat—no matter the cost? We know the story about how the good get it in the end. We know how the story ended for Martin Luther King, Jr., Gandhi, the nuns in El Salvador, Archbishop Romero. So we are apt to hear this story of Daniel in the lions' den as a mere fairy tale we only wish were true.

But perhaps it is true. Perhaps our skepticism is based, not on our sophisticated revulsion at the fantastic details of this little story, but rather on our defensiveness in knowing that it has been so long since we stood up to the boss, called the hand of our classmates, stood our ground, stiffened our backs, so long since we said No! that we don't want any story that reminds us of how cowardly and compromised we have become.

I have told you an old story about a young person on the way up who ran afoul of the powers that be, but still clung to his crazy conviction that God is good, God is just. In the darkness, in the loneliness that results from righteous conviction asserted in the face of stifling conformity, do not fear.

For all you young women and men on the way up, for all of you who are at the top, this story has four points:

1. They will try to do you in; they are out to get you.
2. They are out to get you because moral mediocrity hates moral excellence, and enslaved keepers of the rules can't stand anyone running around loose and free because of conviction.
3. Nobody, not even a king, can save you from tough moral choices.
4. You are vulnerable to the lions and their keepers, *except for God.* Nothing can defeat the relentless moral purposes of God (see Rom. 8). Nothing and nobody.

11

The Writing on the Wall

"You have praised the gods of silver and gold . . . which do not see or hear or know; but the God in whose power is your very breath, and to whom belong all your ways, you have not honored." . . . That very night Belshazzar . . . was killed.

Daniel 5:23*c*, 30*a*

Read Daniel 5:1-17, 23-30.

RABBI HAROLD KUSHNER'S *When Bad Things Happen to Good People* was a religious publishing sensation. Yet many believe that Rabbi Kushner failed to address the toughest moral issue: *Why on earth good things happen to bad people!*

One reason we love Bible stories like the one about Daniel is that the people get what they deserve—a rare occurrence in real life, but an almost everyday one in the Bible, particularly in the book of Daniel. In real life, real creeps are rarely visibly and swiftly punished. Creeps are elected to public office, become presidents of large corporations, pastors of large churches.

But in the Bible, creeps are incinerated in fiery furnaces, eaten by lions, drowned in floods, decapitated. And don't fool yourself, you love that, because everybody loves to see justice done, even if its workings are bloody—maybe particularly if it is bloody, because justice is so rare in real life. But the stories of the Bible often let some creep strut a bit on the stage, do his stuff, then zap! A flood, a lion, the ax falls. How good to see the bad get what they deserve!

In the book of Daniel we meet King Belshazzar, who has thrown a great party for a thousand of his cronies. And in chapter 5, verse 2, we read that "under the influence of the wine," Belshazzar gets a great idea. "Go get me those gold vessels, yea, the ones we stole from the Jewish temple when we ransacked Jerusalem." And he drinks from the sacred vessels in order to mock these impotent Jews, to make fun of their silly God, to show how great Belshazzar is.

And "immediately" (Don't you just love the timing in the Bible? You don't have to wait for the ax to fall, the noose to tighten. It happens immediately.) this great, detached, grisly hand begins writing in large letters on the wall. And the king's mocking, self-assured, arrogant smile is changed. Everyone in the great hall can hear his royal knees knocking together in terror. He calls all his enchanters and diviners to read the writing on the wall, and they can't make out a word of it! They're not worth the money the king pays them.

The queen, a kind of Lady Macbeth figure, says, "O King! Stand up and act like a man! Stiffen your resolve. Go call the exiled Jew, little Daniel. He's good at reading dreams and figuring out weird things."

Daniel is brought into the banquet hall. "So, you are the smart kid, Daniel. I've heard about you, kid. Interpret the writing on the wall, and I'll give you a whole new wardrobe, with jewelry, and a cushy government job."

And Daniel says, "You can keep your job, king. But I'll read the words on the wall."

But before he reads, little Daniel launches into an unbelievable tirade against the king. He tells him that God gave his father, Nebuchadnezzar, a long leash to act as he pleased, but when he got too big for his britches, "his glory was stripped from him," and God made an ass of him (vv. 20-21).

Then he turns on the king before him: "You, Belshazzar . . . have exalted yourself against the Lord of heaven! . . . You and your lords, your wives and your concubines have been drinking wine" from the sacred vessels of Israel. It was the handwriting on the wall.

Daniel reads the words written by the mysterious hand—MENE, MENE, TEKEL, PARSIN—translated as: God says that the time is up for you and your arrogant kingdom. God has weighed you in the scales and found you a lightweight. Your kingdom will be given to others.

Little Daniel has become a prophet, speaking God's truth to power. Belshazzar kept his part of the bargain. He gave little Daniel a new wardrobe, a gold chain, and a good paying government job.

And "that very night Belshazzar . . . was killed" (v. 30). That's the nice thing about this part of the Bible; you don't have to wait long for these divine judgments. The good (little Daniel) get a new suit and a gold chain. The bad (Belshazzar) get to be food for worms, victim of the handwriting on the wall.

You don't believe this story? We are modern people who don't trust the handwriting on the wall. That is, we doubt the possibility of swift, sure retribution or reward. Rabbi Kushner tells us why the good are so rarely rewarded, the evil so seldom punished. We believe in the message of Job. That is, we make much out of the observation that righteous rebels like little Daniel more often get the noose than a gold chain and a promotion, and scumbags like Belshazzar get away with it. Sometimes we whine to God that this is so, but we all seem quite comfortable with the realization that it is so. And so we turn up our noses at this primitive story of the king who shakes before the writing on the wall. This is not the way the world works.

But sometimes it does. Not as often, say, as in the first six chapters of the book of Daniel, to be sure, but sometimes there really does seem to be a kind of justice built into life, a kind of moral law to which we must answer. Odd how that scares us.

A doctor told me that about 80 percent of all visits to the doctor are for lifestyle reasons. I'm not arguing for any *simple* moral cause-effect in life, but still, there do seem to be wages for much of our sin. Something within us tries to deny this. I have never seen a parishioner in the hospital suffering from lung cancer or emphysema who was there because of smoking. They were always there for the kind of lung cancer or emphysema that is caused by something other than smoking.

I didn't say that we *always* reap what we sow. But it is curious how often we do. There is something about us modern people that makes us deny any moral cause-and-effect in life, any modicum of justice built into the world.

The story of Daniel interpreting the king's dream invites us to admit that sometimes—not always by any means, but sometimes—there is, for each of us, the "handwriting on the wall," in which we do reap what we have sown, that prophetic, truthful moment when we realize that our chickens have come home to roost, and justice is done. One of the worst aspects of justice is that time when we actually receive some of it, and the handwriting on the wall is for us!

A friend told me about an acquaintance of his who had just died. He said, "We lived close to each other as boys. I often envied him. He was good-looking, smart, great at tennis, the girls loved him. When we went to college, he rarely had to study to get good grades. I was troubled by the way he treated the women he dated. He was one of those people who always felt the rules were made for everyone but him. He carried that attitude past college into his first marriage. Left his wife and child by age thirty. A succession of affairs followed. He was, we were not surprised to find, quite a wheeler-dealer in business as well as in his personal life.

"On my last trip home, I was told that he had died in a shabby old house near our childhood neighborhood. Life had caught up with him, they say. He died alone, cared for by his old aunt, the last friend he had left in the world."

I suppose that those of us who are not attractive, not good in tennis or adultery, should take heart from that story, that image of a fallen man, forced to a lonely death, gazing at the writing on the wall. But I don't take much comfort in the story, as little as I take in the story of Daniel and Belshazzar. For if it is true, as I think the story in Daniel 5 claims it to be, that God is not mocked, that we are forever accountable for our lives and the way we live them, then I have plenty of reason, like King Belshazzar, to tremble. For there is the possibility of handwriting on the wall for me—I, who in my affluence, power, arrogance, and smug sense of security, more resemble King Belshazzar than poor little exiled Daniel.

All of us have heard the message of Job, that there is no necessary connection between the good we do and the good that happens to us (or vice versa). But have we the imagination to hear *this* message, that "what comes round, comes back around," that "you reap what you sow," that the hand that writes upon the wall is God's, and the prophetic message is a wake-up call for us? This old story bears a message that is simple, proverbial, and often *true.* Is it really so surprising that we love the message of Rabbi Kushner and his interpretation of Job—the message that, sorry, the world is a mess, morally confusing, with the evil getting ahead and the good getting a hard time—more than the message of Daniel to rich, powerful Belshazzar, that God is not forever mocked?

Early in my ministry, my wife, Patsy, and I went to the funeral of a relative of someone in our church. It was in a little country church, a denomination and style of worship different from ours. During the funeral sermon, the preacher emphasized, "It's too late for old Joe. He's dead! He might have wanted to give his life to God, to join the church. Can't now. He's dead!" I thought to myself, What a comfort this must be to the grieving family! "Joe's time is up. But your time, brothers and sisters, is not up. If you are going to give your life to God, do it today. If you are going to get your life right, do it now. There is still time!"

That sermon bothered me. On the way home, I was telling Patsy how insensitive it had been. She agreed. It was insensitive.

"And worst of all," she said, "it was *true.*"

12

The Seduction of Dreams

But the LORD was with Joseph and showed him steadfast love.

Genesis 39:21*a*

Read Genesis 39.

WHEN I WAS A FRESHMAN, the Dean gave a talk at one of our required Tuesday Chapels. He retold that story from *The Odyssey*, in which Odysseus and his men must sail past an island where the Sirens live. The Sirens were those alluring women who sang such beautiful songs that sailors, seduced by their singing, forgot that they were sailing and perished as their ships were dashed against the rocks.

Then the Dean asked, "What songs did the Sirens sing?" And we freshmen knew that he was speaking to us. What songs did they sing? What tune carries you away, seduces you so that you forget where you're going? What song did the Sirens sing? I suppose that for each of us, they sing a different tune. Money. Comfort. Popularity. Sex. Ah yes, isn't it interesting that when we speak of ourselves being detoured, drawn away from the direction we meant to follow, we often speak in terms of *seduction?*

Let me introduce you to Joseph, a young adult with a dream. His daddy and his older brothers didn't particularly like Joseph's dreams, a dream of their bowing down to him, a dream that he was born to rule. That's how Joseph wound up in Egypt as a slave. "Let's do away with this dreamer!" his brothers had said, and they sold their own brother into Egyptian slavery in their attempt to kill the dream.

A young adult with a dream, particularly if it is a big, outrageous dream, can be a real nuisance for the rest of us. Joseph's eleven brothers couldn't have a little brother running around loose among them with so royal a dream.

But we are told, "The LORD was with Joseph, and he became a successful man" (39:2). His was not just any dream, editorializes the writer. It was a dream from God. God has put into this little slave's brain a very big dream. What will happen now? How will this little dreamer from a ragtag nomadic family of sheepherders prosper in great big, cultured Egypt?

Here lies the tension in this story. On the one side, you have little, enslaved Joseph, who has nothing to call his own but a dream, a dream that already has separated him from his family, a troublesome, demanding dream. On the other side, you have Egypt the Empire, the greatest, most powerful, technologically sophisticated far-flung empire the world had known in tenth-century B.C. Who will seduce whom? The great big empire, or the little slave with a dream?

As a slave, Joseph's talents for leadership are immediately recognized. Potiphar, one of Pharaoh's officials, puts Joseph in charge of his house and property. Evidently, Joseph's dream of rulership is not without possibility. See?He's already in charge, even as a young slave.

Mrs. Potiphar sees even more possibility in young Joseph. "Come lie with me!" she demands.

She sees potential in Joseph, potency, power. But like most people who run empires, Mrs. Potiphar misunderstands what real power is about. She is a person who is accustomed to getting what she wants, and now she wants Joseph. "Lie with me!" The orders of a nobleman's wife to a mere slave thus embody the tension between the demands of the empire and the dreams of the slave. It is typical of the imperial, manipulative way of doing business. Will Joseph realize his dream of ruling, or will he be only a plaything of powerful people?

"Joseph, don't you like it here with us in the palace? We have great meals up here at the big house, sleep on satin sheets. It would be a shame for you to have to go back to the dormitory with the other slaves. Speaking of satin sheets. Come lie with me!"

Here the story invites an excursis on the ways the empire uses sex as part of its machinery of enslavement. In the empire, sex most often is considered mainly as of anesthetic value, another only momentarily effective narcotic. If we can convince you, in TV ads, movies, or even university courses on gender, that sex is so very, very important, then maybe we can distract you from thinking about and analyzing the many ways the empire has got you.

Now this ancient teller of the Joseph story writes about another way. See? Mrs. Potiphar presumes that she is so powerful that she can do anything she wants with anybody she wants. Her demand of Joseph, "Come lie with me!" is but another expression of her lust—not for sex, but for power. But in Joseph's refusal, "My master . . . has put everything that he has in my hand. . . . How then could I do this great wickedness, and sin against God?" (39:8*c*-9*c*), we are made to ask, What is real power?

His master's wife, who was supposed to have such power, is reduced to the level of a beggar, pursuing Joseph all day: "Come lie with me! Come lie with me!"

Telegram for Joseph from Potiphar's wife: "Dear Joseph. Stop. Come lie with me. Stop. Love, Mrs. Potiphar." Finally, grabbing his coat, she is left with nothing but his coat as Joseph flees the house.

Clothes have come up in the Joseph story before. Remember Joseph's coat with long sleeves? We were led to believe that it was his royal coat that made little Joseph so special. But now we find that he is royal, even without his clothes. Potiphar's forlorn wife has nothing left in her clutches but his clothes. The real Joseph, the royal Joseph, has resisted, refused her. He is free. Now she is trapped. She will pitifully attempt to use his clothes as evidence against him, in her later lies about Joseph to her husband.

The story is an invitation for you and me to ponder the seductive ways of the empire—the way it wants to kill godly dreams.

Will Joseph forget the dream of God's family when he is in Egypt, once he stops singing Israeli folk tunes and learns to appreciate the cultured music of the palace, the Siren-songs of Imperial Egypt?

No. Four times, the narrator repeats, "The LORD was with Joseph" (39:2, 3, 21, 23), virtually the only times God's name is mentioned in the whole Joseph saga. The Lord is with him. He will not be seduced by the empire.

"Come on, Joseph, you'll find that people do things a bit differently here in Palm Beach."

Some scholars think that this story was told during imperial time in Israel, during the great age of King Solomon, when at last Israel had power, as other nations name power, a time of great national self-confidence and pride, a new world order with Israel at the top. Prosperity. A good defense program. And I think this story was meant to make Israel reconsider what real power is. Is it power to go with the flow, find out which tunes are most accepted by those at the top, and then to dance to that beat? Or is real power a by-product of people who have a dream and will not be seduced out of that dream? I think the story was meant to say that Israel has power because "the Lord was with Joseph."

When you stand before the seductive wiles of the empire—the modern corporation, the university, your first law firm—it is great power to know that *they don't own you.*

A friend of mine was a student at Duke University in the mid-sixties, which is significant because my friend is African American, and Duke had been racially integrated only a couple of years before he enrolled. He was the first person in his family to go to college. Can you imagine the power of the godly dream that propels someone that far? Well, when he got to Duke, he discovered that, though he was ready to work on his dream, Duke was not in all ways ready for him. In the late sixties, he became part of a protest against certain practices at Duke. There was a strike, tension.

His parents pled with him, "Son, keep things in perspective. You are lucky just to be there at that big university. You'll do well to forget this protest business, go study hard, and get your degree. Be careful!" They knew that the empire can be ruthless with those who don't go with the flow.

But he had a dream, a dream bigger than Duke, bigger even than the dreams of his own parents for him, bigger certainly than what the empire was then ready to offer. He had a dream that God was with him, and he refused to be seduced. He is now a professor, head of African American studies at Duke Divinity School.

Or should we say that *God*, in God's dream, had him?